# PRAYERS FOR THE
# DEAD VENTRILOQUIST
by
## D.J. Smith

## Ahsahta Press
Boise State University
Boise, Idaho

# Acknowledgments

Grateful acknowledgment is made to the editors of the following magazines in which the poems in this volume have appeared or will appear : *Alabama Literary Review, The Antigonish Review, The Birmingham Poetry Review, Carolina Quarterly, Florida Review, Folio, Green Mountain Review, Hiram Poetry Review, Laurel Review, The Madison Review, Mid-America Review, Minnesota Review, Mississippi Valley Review, New Virginia Review, Passages North, Poetry Canada Review, The Quarterly, South Dakota Review, South Florida Review, Southern Poetry Review, Stand, Tar River Poetry Review,* and *Zone 3*.

I would also like to thank Peter Everwine, Corrinne Hales, Charles Hanzliceck, Dorianne Laux, and Philip Levine.

Editor for Ahsahta Press: Dale K. Boyer

*Prayers for the Dead Ventriloquist*
is printed on acid-free text and cover papers.

ISBN 0-916272-62-1

Library of Congress Catalog Card Number:
94-73339

# Contents

Introduction *by Dorianne Laux* ..........................................iii

# I

Fire ........................................................................3
Psalms......................................................................4
Easter, 1960 ...............................................................6
Storm Birds.................................................................7
The Blackcrowned Sparrow....................................................8
The Ditch...................................................................9
Sister.....................................................................11
Winter Memory .............................................................12
Song of My Brother ........................................................13
Amos, Who Says to Tell Everybody He's Still Making
   It Somewhere in Rural California .......................................14
Prayers for the Dead Ventriloquist ........................................15
There Was a Tree ..........................................................17
Fear ......................................................................18
Men .......................................................................20
Gasoline ..................................................................21
Ghost .....................................................................22
Available Light............................................................23
Desire.....................................................................24
In the Brief Light of Summer ..............................................25
The Good Child.............................................................26
Requiem for the Unborn ....................................................27

# II

Sparrow....................................................................31
December Evening...........................................................32
Pilgrim....................................................................35
Faith......................................................................36
The Witness ...............................................................37
Wild Chrysanthemums .......................................................38
The Sleepers ..............................................................40
What is Necessary..........................................................41
Washington Square, San Francisco...........................................42
Midnight Outside the Transbay Terminal ....................................44
For the Paraplegic Woman Who Lives Above Me ...............................45

Maggie's Legacy ........................................................................46
The Quiet Ambition of Grass ...................................................47
Night Song ................................................................................48
Everywhere the Light ...............................................................49
Three Times I Petition the Sky ...............................................51
Hummingbird ...........................................................................52

# III

Beauty .......................................................................................57
Eyes of Winter ..........................................................................59
Prayer for the Living ................................................................60
On the Morning of Your New Life ..........................................62
The Wrecking Yard ...................................................................63
The Fine Art Cinema ................................................................65
Near Treeline ............................................................................67
Jimmy Finds-A-Feather Speaks for Me ...................................69
The Marrying Poem ..................................................................71
One Day at a Time ....................................................................72
Blood Rings ..............................................................................73

# Introduction

There is a certain kind of darkness that invites us in, illuminates, then opens again into another darkness that pulses with its own invitation and illumination. This is also true of a certain kind of poetry, poems that, as they open, one into another, lead us through a maze of shadowy corridors and wrong turns, well-crafted, precise, intelligent poems we remember and learn from.

Van Gogh once wrote to his brother, Theo, "One of the most beautiful things is to paint darkness with light in it." A task that sounds easier than it is. D. J. Smith's first book is built, poem by poem, into a complex network of families and failures, beehives, pale birches, love, hope, dust and blood, loneliness, and light: the stale, sodden light of summers, the short, sharp light of winters, the unnatural "boxed light" of cities. In "Psalms," he writes:

> I rode a bus full of people
> flushed with aquarium light,
> through the tunnel of a city
> and I wondered if that city
> could feel the needle of our
> loneliness passing through
> its great heart.

That needle of light and loneliness is driven through this book, its pointed question, its accurate vision. This is not an easy book. Little relief is offered in these poems. A dark apparition begins to rise in childhood as a boy views his world and begins to comprehend it:

> Only a few feet below
> the bright streets of my
> neighborhood I could find
> the lost cats, fur shivering
> with flies, the sodden mattress,
> the fish heads, iridescent,
> half rotted and stinking.
> I knew that here once,
> in the dark opened throat
> of an overpass, a girl had been raped.
> Even then I could imagine

                    her love forced open
                    and hammered like her head
                    against the concrete piling.

    These poems are prayers both for and against the darkness, prayers intoned as Smith looks hard, as all poets should, at what is placed before him, whatever unfolds and falls under any beam of available light. This harsh, particular light falls first on the people who pass through his smaller world: a mother working silently at her job, a father reading the Bible, a sister who wakes from nightmares, a brother who takes his knack for violence off to a war that will place a metal plate beneath his skull and swallow his soul. It's the child in the middle, the quiet one, who sees and records and labors to make sense of the chaos, whose sense of self reminds me a little of the James Agee character who comprehensively inhabits the world of adulthood and death—"successfully disguised to myself as a child." As the child grows, the larger family of humanity is revealed and preserved. These are people we recognize in these poems, their stoppered lives: Amos, a retired Army vet who tells a war story the poet wants not to hear or have to imagine or write about, the truth forced on him as certain truths are forced on us, or into us, or pulled groaning from within us, Amos, who admonishes the poet, challenges him, shouting, "Hell, it's the truth./Put *that* in your poem." And Smith does, because he takes these people seriously, their pain and their pleasure, their tenuous truths, shining his own steady light on the paraplegic woman who sketches pigeons; Maggie, who allows men to visit her body for a mere forty dollars; Jimmy Finds-a-Feather, who understands what it is to be "at the very center of things"; or the man who hangs himself in his barn, his widow sounding her high-pitched grief as the owl looks on; the woman in the Raider's T-shirt and blue panties who runs in the yard to call her cat; the old man next door, dying of cancer:

                    He'd sit in his yard, in what was left
                        of the body that rotted

                    around him like a piece of bad fruit. And while
                        I watched he'd wink
                    and stuff the butt of a Camel filter into a hole
                        no more the thickness
                    of a child's finger, slit by surgeons in his throat.
                        Mostly I remember
                    how he closed his eyes when he did it.

iv

How it gave him
pleasure.

And surrounding them all, "sparrows clutching" the trees, "rain eating holes in the snow," "clumps of doves," daffodils blooming through the bones of a deer, bodies of water, grasses, thin trees, and light: sunlight, starlight, moonlight; the natural world provided not as solace, as savior, but as reflector, quiet backdrop to the suffering of our animal lives, lives built on the smallest of pleasures, the simplest of lies. As these lives accumulate around us, we begin to see ourselves in each of them, "curious and dumb," like the boy on the corner waiting for a bus, "young enough to be a little ashamed/of his mother," a little stunned to be alive admidst so much ragged beauty and exquisite pain. And the hope and love that is found and offered is not trite, but born of reality's capacity to astonish: "And though I would not choose my life/I am often surprised by it." From that surprise comes a tentative reconciliation with the world, the fractured self:

It is what kept me
Standing there in town,
In the mirror's three
Versions of myself,
Measured for the second
Suit I've owned, beautiful
Enough to marry.

It's said that, because there was no moon, Van Gogh painted "Starry Night" with candles stuck in his hat band. This book has that feel, that kind of blurred swirl, a hard-won beauty that emerges from a patient struggle with the dark, so that we are as surprised as the poet at how "love can come/To live inside you/Long after you stopped/Wanting it," at how "You could look back/And call it luck."

*Dorianne Laux*
Eugene, Oregon
December, 1994

for my family

# I

*Threads of light attach*
*at the shoulders of her silk kimono.*
*From the balcony she's yelling at her man*
*in the street. This morning*
*it's her red hair that saves me.*
*And the green snake*
*that grows from her feet.*

# Fire

Winter strings its web of darkness
while the wind threatens the windows,
fringed with ice. In their castles
bees are drowsing, combing woodsmoke
from their woolen, buffalo heads.
The sky empty of birds.
Still, light thrills the spines
of birches and your hands
bathe in the heat of coals.
Soon spring will come and
flies will dust the backs of animals.
Everything changes, except this hunger.
Look, the fire tastes
the plum's branches. Deeper,
in the heartwood, lies the sweetness.

# Psalms

## I.

I think it was a mosquito,
a little wing'ed god, a furious humming
as it drowned there in the canals of blood.
I think it was his dying
that half-roused me, that sang in my ear.
It was the same sound I heard
in the trees as a child
when I felt separate
from my family. Once, then,
I rode a bus full of people
flushed with aquarium light,
through the tunnel of a city
and I wondered if that city
could feel the needle of our
loneliness passing through
its great heart. I think it could.
Even now, when I lie
awake to the syllables of this rain
at the window, or walking
some avenue I feel a sharpness in my chest,
I ask, Who has passed there?
Was it my brother? Or my
mother? Was that my father,
just now, entering the world.

## II.

I remember little
of what my father said,
though surely he must have
spoken. What remains
is his strong sweet odor,
the liver spots on his hands,
how the light struck
his translucent blue eyes.

Memory stumbles
on a road with the sharp smell
of sourgrass
blowing up from the river
the way it would summers
when we'd drive out
of the city's boxed light.
A blue Mercury
station wagon, high-finned
and white-walled,
wallowing through the evening
hills, our ten heads bobbing.
Each a black seed
of silence, each so young
and poor and dumb. I remember
rain smeared the windshield
and his face set hard, his
streaming blue eyes staring
past the wipers clacking quietly.
Wondering, I thought, like all
of us, *Which road*
*could have brought us*
*to such loneliness? Which*
*would lead us out?*

# Easter, 1960

In this memory I'm 5 & standing
In the sun with my sister & father
As if facing a camera. It's Easter &
My father & I sport white sweaters
And matching bow ties. He's a small man
And stands a little behind us, hands
At his side, his forehead & his eyes
Gleaming with perspiration. He wants to
Smile, you can tell he wants to, it's not his
Fault, it's the light, it's coming
Down & he can't do anything but
Force the muscles of his face back.
My sister & I look chubby,
A little pale. We're squinting
Too & holding each other's hands
So tightly our knuckles whiten
Where the blood refuses its flesh.

# Storm Birds

I recognize these mammoth trees
that come to the window,
shaggy and blind with age,
sparrows clutching their sides.

When I was young
my mother's hair, cropped
short, felt like grass
against my face.
In her voice
I always heard
the cry of gulls.

For years she lived alone
in a house with a man
whose silence outlived him.
It was a keepsake sewn
into the lining of her coat,
and the seams on my sister's wrist,
the black threads of this page.

Yesterday I heard birds
blown inland by a storm
and saw her out
of the corner of my eye,
kneeling in the garden, near
the trees, mud and salt
on her hands, her eyes
shadowed with rain.

# The Blackcrowned Sparrow

When my BB struck
its head with a dull
puffed thud, the sparrow
swung down from the
telephone wire like
a gymnast dismounting
in a straight dead
fall to the patio
where my mother sat
absorbing the summer
light and morning paper.
Startled, she stared
at the blood
beading like jam
on its blackhooded crown.
She said nothing,
folded her paper
methodically and
looked at her hands,
salmon pink in the sun,
left me alone —
my shadow as still
as that small bird
spoiling darkly
the bright cement.

# The Ditch

As a boy I was taken
with the way in winter
the ditches around my house
would dry out and open
like graves for everything
dead or abandoned.
Only a few feet below
the bright streets of my
neighborhood I could find
the lost cats, fur shivering
with flies, the sodden mattresses,
the fishheads, iridescent,
half rotted and stinking.
I knew that here once,
in the dark opened throat
of an overpass, a girl had been raped.
Even then I could imagine
her love forced open
and hammered like her head
against the concrete piling.

Evenings, my mother,
tired with work, would
speak softly to herself
as my father, who
spoke to no one,
moved his lips carefully
over the black
words in his Bible.
I remember the television
flickering quietly
with the blurred light
of a war I knew
had swallowed my brother.
I'd walk away
from that house under
a dusk sky swollen
purple, darkness falling

slowly around me, and
I would climb down
and enter the earth.

# Sister

She has moved
past the common loneliness
of pensioners boring the sales clerks
at Macy's, through the parks
and the spotted autumn trees.
Sometimes she stops, and lets
the leaves swirl in a flurry
at her feet. She thinks
that without them, she could not endure
the steady eyes of doormen,
the long months of snow to come.

In her room she works
a torn sheet into the cracks
where tonight the wind
will wear at the window
and remembers the water
running slowly in the tub.
How it sounds, she writes,
like someone's thoughts spilling
towards a conclusion. I am frightened
by her letters.

Last night I dreamt
of the slow migration
of birds, of the child
that grew into a stranger.
She was always quiet
like this morning's rain
eating holes in the snow.
There were nights she'd stand,
motionless in the doorway
of my room, terrified
that somewhere within her
a black seam was
leaking. I never said, *Don't go*.

# Winter Memory

Last night the plumbing choked.
Now the driveway's ice, lacquered
Black. A clump of doves breaks
From the telephone pole, a hushed
Cross raised over the road.
I see the holes where snow's
Collapsed, my father's eyes,
The year my brother left.

# Song of My Brother

Because you cannot sleep, or listen any longer
To the flies gone mad on the sill,
You edge toward the corner
Of the bed, pulling each sock on, carefully,
Without thought of the bitter wind
That rose last night, a dark
Wing over the valley. You stood
For a long time watching
The thin palms of the boulevard
Shudder and bow. And the years lost
Digging line in the desert
For Pacific Gas and Electric
Came back to you,
How the winds there struck
With the sudden concussion of a shell.

       You walk out
Under a sky, blank and sticky, laden
With the odors of spring, a sky
You told me once, you saw in its entirety
In the loose eyes of a dead coyote.
Though you know it was there, in the quiet,
Unblinking face of a Laotian streetwalker
The day you struggled to leave yourself
In her.

Each day you walk a little farther
Not knowing whether you move
Away or towards.
In the dry heat of this afternoon
You drink to dignity
And silence
With the Indians and hard-core Okies
In Ray Caveros's West Side Bar.
And as the alcohol begins its slow erasure
You hear the blood
Singing over the metal plates
In your skull, and you think,
This is not your home. It never was.

# Amos, Who Says Tell Everybody He's Still Making It Somewhere in Rural California

Amos lives alone
in a single-wide trailer, propped
in the corner of a 5 acre plot
of scrub oak and beer cans. He's retired,
Army, 20 years of yes sirs and close
quarters, the singular odor of men.
He's seen oil slicks burn huge halos
over the Mekong, left two fingers
in the snows of Korea, knows
gooks are tough. Don't let anybody kid
you, he says, tenacious as rust.
The women, they're tighter. No shit,
ask anyone. Christ, once we played
poker, while these girls, kids really,
knelt under the table. One for each
of us, for a quarter. Imagine, a quarter.
And I do for a second see it
in the hands of a girl, in the smoked light
of a grass house, a coin of the first world,
bearing the likeness of a dead revolutionary.
She places it in the hands of her mother, and
the mother takes it because she must. And
then I don't want to imagine it anymore nor even be
there, and stumble off through the doveweed
and dirt hearing him shout, Hell, it's the truth.
Put *that* in your poem.

# Prayers for the Dead Ventriloquist

Sometimes I waken early with a mind as slow
as an ice field breaking up after winter, a memory
moving out on each chunk of snow.
I go downtown to buy the silence
of waiters, the first lights of the city, the window
where I watch a sky painted today
with the gravity of rain. A man
standing on the sidewalk seems unable or unwilling
to move, the way standing in some museums
I've wanted to walk into the landscape
of a city but just stood there, knowing
it was enough to take that city
into me. A street magician is setting
up on the corner, checking his scarves
and his flowers, his coat of many colors.
He reminds me of the ventriloquist
the nuns hired once on the Feast
of the Transfiguration of Christ
to entertain the children of St. Theresa's —
the little flowers of Jesus of whom I was one.
He was an old man, an immigrant from Chile,
who could pass his spirit with ease into the body
of his lap companion. And when that wooden boy
sang a song of his homeland, of the devil's tails
that swept out over the roads as night
closed its circle, of a boy walking home
by the light of a lantern, light in his heart,
we felt his longing deepen its route
as it swept through us, until some cried
and we all applauded with abandon. I remember
the eyes of that boy, swiveling wildly
when his father stood up, tearing at his collar,
his eyes filling with surprise and curiosity
as he collapsed on the floor of his last performance,
the felt curtains scurrying closed. The whole
school knelt to say the rosary as, once only,
we had knelt when the President was killed
and the nuns wept openly. I wondered

what would become of that boy, lying
closed in a suitcase, the songs buried
in his heart. Even now, sometimes
when I close my eyes to this city
and what it has become, I hear a voice
full of hope and longing, a lantern
swinging toward me in the dark.

# There Was a Tree

A eucalyptus, so old that
from what looked like its
third story rose a grove
of smaller trees, the watery light
running over the leaves. When
evening came, starlings would infest
it, black rags caught in the fluttering
branches.

        Sometimes
I stood on the roots that lifted
from the grass, the way I had
stood on the scuffed brogues
of my uncle when we danced
across the linoleum in his room
at the Veteran's Hospital. He died
there in the winter of '62, thinned
by alcohol and grief for a life
lived alone. I was seven.

I would cling
to the bark of that trunk, feel
the tree take the wind, tossing
its great head as if it begged to be
cut loose. As if it begged.

# Fear

Today a cold wind
piles leaves
around the rotting plums
and the weeds of the driveway.

Almost forty,
my brother wears away
another long weekend
in the shadow of a rusting
Austin-Healey.

Fear and anger
locked his jaw and hunched his back
years ago. Behind thick glasses
his eyes still appear

too near, too hungry.
My neighbor, the new wife, bangs
out her back door in a Raider's T-
shirt and blue panties; she folds
her arms to hold herself, shivering

and hissing, *Shit!* Raised on toes
painted the color of cranberries
she calls out for her cat. Hearing her
my brother crawls out

from under the frozen motor.
She is bowing to uncoil
the smooth rope of hair, knotted
just above the back of her neck.
She shakes slowly, letting it

unfold to her shoulders
where it quivers with sun.
She looks hard at the trees
and we look with her

and in the spaces among leaves
see what light shines there.
Later, he'll want to break
for a beer and the sure pleasure
of a Lucky, smoked

reverently with the half-lidded
eyes of a lover. *Ah, hell,* he'll
say as always, *Someday,*
*this wreck will go.*

# Men

I sit with my back to the wall
at the end of a coffee shop
chewing the doughy pastry and watching
the old men, hunched over the counter.

I've seen them walking the parks
beneath the war memorials and clock towers.
Sometimes stray bits of paper
run at their heels like small dogs.

Sometimes they just sit
until the sun moves and they go
to their rooms
or to a cafe on a lighted avenue

like this. And I am made
grateful by the miles and the years,
the losses that separate
me from them,

by the woman who sleeps
in my bed and wakes
to my needs. Still,
there is something

in me which darkens
as it feeds
from the same heart,
its bitter root.

# Gasoline

I've broken down with my bike again
Near Belmont and Church
Under a glass sky chilled
By night wind
And the last of this morning's stars.
A man spots me and crosses
The street, smelling of gasoline
And stands coughing, so close to me
I can hear his lungs rattle and crack
And imagine the cells down there,
A cluster of blackberries, rotted
And splitting. He stands there
Watching me, his knees going soft,
Buckled by wind and too much wine.
He wants the 50 cents I won't
Give him. One of his eyes
Is sick and so pale, that for a second,
I see the host the priests of my youth
Would loft as I rang the bells
And mouthed the secret Latin sounds.
He wants to talk, says just last week
A woman with two children
Parked her van right there near
The alley and doused herself
With gasoline, screaming about sin
And the sure power of immolation.
He doesn't know why it happened.
"What do you think?" he says, "Was it love
Or terror that made her kids
Stay still?" "I don't know," I say,
As I eye the sun beginning
To leach through the strata
Of clouds on the horizon. It strikes
Our faces and warms them
As finally the bike sputters,
Catches fire and holds.

# Ghost

We lifted our oars and drifted
in a circle,
in the slow
revolution of fall
as the water of the cove
streaked with violet and blue
went black, and the trees
gathered around us, inked
against the sky.
Venus nailed herself
to a roof of stars. It was
so still, I could hear you
breathing. Later,
I woke.

Tonight I lie awake
and listen to my wife
breathe
in the struggling rhythm
of dream.
I know that you are living.
It's spring again, and boys
are killing themselves in the streets.
They spray fences
with marks of their territory, the walls
with the names
they would have us remember.

# Available Light

She came the year I lay exhausted by my life
In my small white rooms off the boulevard.
She talked about restraint in love,
what it takes to get it right,
how the first lines must drop, true
as a stone sinks in water, how
one good line is worth the time
of its thousand poorer brothers.
I lay waiting for her, though I did not know it then,
behind those windows without blinds, the broken chest
spilling soiled laundry. She told me when her Michael
died, that it was strange that she felt
anger toward a God that didn't exist.
I think now of her face, how it really was
a child's face, a rural, mystic, child, held
half in the dark like one of the ruined figures
in her black and white portraits
made in available light.

# Desire

Pale moonlight falls
Through the window as
The dust glinting like sequins
Twists slowly in the air.
You toss your head,
Pick the broken strands
From the brush you dragged
Through your hair
And drop them more easily
Than you will a moment like
This. Stepping out of your
Jeans, pooled on the floor
You leave for now the life
You have known to bring
Me the scent of rain and soil
From the garden where
Today you planted the first
Dark seeds that will grow
Into tomatoes.
You will serve them
From cool plates this summer
To your husband and watch
As he chews them with
Simple appreciation, beads
Of sweat gathering on his
Lip, and you will wonder
What is in him that is so
Still and so easily satisfied.
But now as I plant kisses
On your delicate white shoulders
I pass beyond thinking, see
My hand trace the slender
Bow of your hip, touching
The place where our
Lives grow together,
Pressed closer than
We would have planned.

# In the Brief Light of Summer

Only the echo of a jay
follows me
through the trees where
high above a creek
I watch a young girl
stepping into the water, shining
like a bed of silver coins

catching the light.
The long wet
hair she twists
in a black rope falls
over her shoulders
touching one breast,
the delicate bones of her back

curving in a long question.
I can feel the chill of water
as it slides along her leg
and the sun washing her neck.
(In what hour did I grow old?)
Swirled, split by rocks —
dropped into a deep pool

the stream goes on
making the sound of rain.
When I close my eyes,
the rustle of birds
comes to me like remembered love,
weaving a nest, pulling
the dry grass through my heart.

# The Good Child

The good child learns
His new father's hands
Are as hard as the fenceposts
Planted out back. Evenings
He sees him slit
The slick throats of
Catfish in the kitchen,
Humming softly to himself.
His mother wears
A smile of cracked china
And spills little kisses
Down his delicate neck.
But a faint odor of fish
Now presses her skin
And her eyes seem pasted on
The way a pigeon's are.
The good child stops crying.
Watching his father's hand
Brush down his small arm,
He says please
And thank you very much.
At night, alone
He stands staring
At his warm piss
Steaming from the rug.
He listens for snow
Collecting quietly
On the roof,
A faucet dripping
Somewhere in the dark.
And wonders if morning
Will bring his mother
New eyes.

# Requiem for the Unborn

The day drops low
into the branches
of the westward trees
as a chill wind crawls forward
under the leaves on the lawn.
And something like my spirit
slides deeper within
as quickly as a figure
slips through a mirror.
I hear my heart
trotting its tiny circle.
What we need to know
comes too late; I can see
my unborn on the beach
of childhood, their bright faces
turned out toward sea, the sun
coming in on the curling waves,
the light, ground like yellow glass,
shining and useless in the sand.

II

# Sparrow

There was a wind
coming in just
before rain that
tossed and buffeted
my car, the long
grass of the plain
whipping back and forth,
the dark clouds swelling
like smoke overhead, a few
fat raindrops slapping
down. Then a sparrow, lost
in the wind-rush, flung
in a wing blur of
feather and light, plunged
headlong, neck-snapped,
against my windshield.
It held there, the force
of the car pressing
its head to one side, its
eye on mine, so that
for a second, it seemed
like the face of a woman
in the moment of love. Then
it dragged across the length
of the window and was
gone. And just for
a moment, somehow,
I did not feel alone, there
in the car with the rain
letting go, the road
signs twisting, the grey
towers of the city, rising
like silos in the distance, me
homing then,
with terrible speed.

# December Evening

The frail light
Of December fades slowly.
Streetlamps wink on and drone
Like cold bees above the empty
Streets. A man in a damp basement
Drops his shirt and trousers
Into the washer and tells himself
Gently, as if to a child,
Yes. This matters.
There are clouds
Shadowing over the roofs of houses
Where no one feels safe,
Where my neighbors go on
Stacking wood against winter.
On an evening like this
I rode a night train
Out of the long shadow
Of the San Joaquin.
Outside my window
Lights flared from the tops
Of slaughterhouses and silos,
Tin cathedrals dropping away
In the distance the way
A man's thoughts
Thin towards sleep.

I lost my way that year,
Giving all of myself to a woman
So that when she brought her lover home
I could do nothing
But go into the street speaking
Softly to myself,
As if to a dog that sensing
An intruder whines and quivers.
Some nights before sleep
I see the handkerchief
Of the old woman who sat alone
On that train, on the edge

Of her seat. For miles she
Coughed into it, until
It was a rose
Crushed in the grey of her hands.

And though I would not choose my life
I am often surprised by it.
I was surprised
By the sudden and complete happiness
Of my mother at the birth
Of my brother, and years later,
Astonished at the rage
With which he drove a fist of nails
Through the long board he swung
With purposeful, athletic grace
Killing our neighbor's
Doberman Pinscher.
I remember the black sack
Of bones he left sagged
In the dirt of an empty lot,
The torn flesh stitched
With a red line of ants,
The loose eyes, the delicate
Curl of the tongue.
For weeks I was fascinated
By the gradual letting go
Of tissue as each separate cell
Gave up its love
Of the body, slowly.
I watched the drowsy kiss
Of the meatbee, the steady
Pillaging of ants, the dust.

So I continue
With the small steamed breaths
I ladle out into evenings like this
When the wind dies
And the wood eaves of this house tick
And suddenly something snaps
Overhead, perhaps a bat
Sure of its purpose.

I wait
For the certain pleasure of the moon
Leaking over the rooftops,
Lighting my face and
The blind eyes of the windows.

# Pilgrim

No eye in the black surf of a storm
rolling in over a wheatfield in what was then Kansas,
just the grass beginning to sway, the starlings
shook loose, bolting
back and forth in the sky,
nervous in their confusion.

I rattle by in a battered pickup,
strings of rain in the truck's mirror.
My breath against the window,
hands dead on the wheel.
Perhaps it's as she told me,
that I've gone bad in the head again.

I'm not sure.
Here within the darkness creeping forward,
are the spells of childhood. Sister
with her new lips and little box
of mother's hair.
Brother who kisses me
and walks away crying.
There I am, running again
down the road
with a dead sparrow
jammed on the end of a stick.

# Faith

The moon slips
Off the roof
Laden with the silence
Of dead seas.
Some nights I am afraid
Of its simplicity.
Some nights I believe
In the power of angels
And dream their quick teeth
Sink in the soft darkening
Fruit of my shoulders.
Some mornings I wish I lived
In the kingdom
Of another man's skin.
Always I dress quickly
For the first rags of sun
And the early crows
Muscling overhead
Slowly clenching and unclenching
Their black-fingered wings.

# The Witness

One night, as a boy of sixteen,
having eaten what I thought
were the holy buds of a cactus,
I lay down in the dark
to give myself over to sleep or to dream
in the upstairs room of my parent's home.
Later I woke
to the sounds of boxcars clicking north in the rain,
the watery threshing of my heart in its pocket
of rain. And as I floated down
toward the eyes, toward the arms and the legs
outflung and lost on the bed,
there was a light
exploding in my head, a rhythmic snapping
of flashbulbs until I was quiet,
a thing of the light.

That night a woman weighed down by
her life, by Seconal and wine, drifted
across Van Ness Boulevard, shot the curb
and crushed to a halt, engine ticking
against the trunk of a eucalyptus.
A boy of sixteen walked out of the rain,
out of the dark, with cobalt eyes
to watch the fire tiptoe
along the headliner, dripping
like a burning candle onto her cheek.
He tried to move, to speak,
but his mouth was useless
and so no sound came; he was lost
in the growing dawn-sea glow
of the windshield, the tiny goat hooves of rain, clattering
over the car top, the shining
iridescence of the street. Still now
when he hears the screams
of sirens at night, he remembers her hair,
the way it rose up just before it burst into light.

# Wild Chrysanthemums

When the dusk light of December bleeds quickly
Clotting in the cold darkening leaves
I go to bed early and lie in wonder
Of an earlier winter & a woman
With delicate blue skin who dropped
One day to the floor of our small
Worn apartment, her eyes as cool
As black marbles, head rocked to one side
Vomiting blood. I remember her face
Opened with surprise, in the way
One might marvel in private
At the disloyalty of friends, as she
Watched bubbles of red saliva pop
And collapse on the thinning
Beige carpet. She believed she was dying
And so told me she loved me
And in the moment I dialed paramedics calmly
I knew it had all been a mistake
And that if she lived I would leave her
Just as I have left other mistakes.

Last spring I stood at a window
And watched wild chrysanthemums struggling
In the wind. They surged in the heat, scratching
The glass and seemed to me somehow
Hardened like bright coral. And I saw
Also out that window a vision
Of childhood, of my father lying
On a made bed, silent. He would lie
So still and stubbornly that I imagined
It was his hope to become stone.
I believed that his anger was because
He felt the burden of his children
Denied him this final, simple desire.
And as I watched him attempt again
His quiet transformation I would feel
A hopelessness rising in me like
Sand filling in my shoes, filling my legs,

Loading my once hollow arms, my small
Afternoon heart clicking quietly until
I grew heavy & wished also to be stone
And gone.

It was in September when I stood
With a dark haired woman & watched
The orange hulls of ships heave steadily
Through the white lashed & black waves
That fill California's great bay.
I was awed by their grand & swift arrival,
By the melodic clang of buoys
And the shrill tickling wind that rushed over me
When I realized I had finally come to love
The random suffering of my life
In the simple way those of us without
Beauty come to love the graceless
Bodies we endure. And if this is
A simplification then let me grow simple
Like the cows on those cold fields
That slope up from the water
Their shoulders circled to the wind
Mooing like sad cellos. Let me believe for awhile
In the gentle laughter this new woman gives me.
This woman who once sold her body for junk.
Whose own sad mistakes have held & pressed
Her dearly. This woman who now
Tugs & sets me lightly
Into streaming blue oceans of sleep.

# The Sleepers

In the beautiful white city
by the bay, people
lie in the park half-dappled
in dusk light, drowsing,

the smell of the sea
and the smell of the leaves
blowing over them.
Some smoke, others speak

to themselves or stare
at the water, the fat ducks
sliding by. A woman lifts
her hair, shakes it free

and stills herself again.
And the light touches
each thing as the eye
falters, and for now they

let go of the world.
Stars rise
above the castles
of their skin.

# What is Necessary

Beneath the cliffs the dirty gulls sweep low
over the dunes at my back. They cry
or shit once, lifting on their shifting
avenues of air. Here, even the clumps of grass
are tentative, their roots clutching
fistfuls of running sand. In the distance
fog burns and the hills surface
humped closely like blue whales.
As a child I'd come here
and trace a circle in the spongy sand
that edges the water. I'd lie down
in its center, close my eyes and let
the ocean rush over me, black and frothy.
I'd hold my breath
until the thousand precise threads
of light flashed over me and the white
water drained slowly away. In my trough,
the wind blowing over me, were my eyes
sheened with wonder? Today the wind
slaps my ears with the snap of a sheet.
And I watch the sea climb out
of its grave, collapse and slip back.

# Washington Square, San Francisco

I remember
The way we fell apart
Into our separate selves,
The surf of our breath breaking
Over the silence
Of that room. The black
At the center of your eyes
Grew large, then still
As your body cooled next to mine,
Until you slept,
And the dusk light
Darkened on the wall.
I lay there for a long while after
Watching spots appear overhead
In the dark, whorling
Like the luminaries
In Van Gogh's Starry Night.
I thought of him then,
Bandaged, penniless and drunk,
His eyes already sick
With the light of
Sunflowers.
Years later I sit on this bench
And smoke, my eyes
Following the woman
Crossing Washington Square.
It is you I am remembering
In a thin dress and sandals
Cutting quickly through the crowd
And the little field of cropped flowers,
Blood red in their buckets.
A man in the street is screaming
In Chinese at the buses droning
Indifferently at the curb.
And the bells wake, finally
In their towers as
The light pours down
As it will. And my eyes

Begin to blur as you are one
More shimmering body in the many,
Your yellow hair flaring,
The rippling of a flower
Or a match struck with wind.

# Midnight Outside the Transbay Terminal

It's the rain
that's made him
leave what he calls
the circle of power,
the circle he traces
each night before sleep.
In this way, he
tells me, the visions
that rise like bubbles
in a man's body
can't corrupt him when
they snap
on the slick surface
of brain.
Still, he says
he sees her
when rain
settles into the graves
in his eyes. She's there
in late September
stepping over the soft
fruit that has
fallen, the split
mouths of pomegranates
open in the grass —
and there always
are the many
white smocked moths
rising in bursts
before her as
she laughs, running
toward the whips
of birches trembling
in their planted
rows of light.

# For the Paraplegic Woman Who Lives Above Me

Nights I hear her wheeling overhead in the ceiling
                        her t.v. screaming
an evangelist's vision.
        Days she comes down
                        in front of the building

        to sketch pigeons
                        that strut there
in gutter pools.
        Later she will paint them
                        with glassy blue throats

        catching the light.
                        On Tuesdays the nurse comes
to bathe her.
        I imagine her dead
                        legs swimming in the tub,

        the pale hands separating
                        the knees, gently
sponging the hollows.
        How she closes her eyes
                        and leans into

        the cold tile.
                        The clear soft water rippling.
And always the insistent
        iridescence. Always
                        the wings stunned with light.

# Maggie's Legacy

This morning another awakening, a few small clouds
Huddled like cobblestones overhead, the day
Dripping cold off the rooftops, and she breathes
In the dampness, the naked light crawling
Over the bed. Is it the rain or the wind
Seeping under the wooden frame of the window
That pulls her toward memory with the rich undertow
Of dreams? It was raining. And her father's
Beard, still wet, felt like grass against
Her neck. And his hands, the fingers he
Clamped over her mouth, smelled of tobacco, so that even
Now, 20 years later, she feels a trembling
In her throat when a man smokes. Last night
The wind blew a few stars in, 40 dollars and a man
Pressing down on her, his hands shaking
Her shoulders as he finished, as if to say,
*Go on, now. Breathe.*

# The Quiet Ambition of Grass

This jay, blue rag of the same sky
that settles around me, screams
at the cat couched in the long summer
grass. I'm half asleep under the elm
feeling its shadow embroider my body.
My shepherd keeps faith at my feet,
his cold nose nuzzling my ankles;
his ears, all hope, black flames
ticked forward and wavering. Red scarf
of a woodpecker flashes above. He's
measuring the length of the future
in steady, hypnotic staccato.
Today I promise myself
I'll move past bitterness and melancholy
for the sarcoma the doctors say
blossoms like black mold across my brain.
I'll read Whitman and let myself feel
the stillness of the garden, beating
with the quiet ambition of grass.
I'll follow this sparrow who cartwheels
once, flits upward and stitches the sky.

# Night Song

I have no pity for the boy I was,
Drifting through the dawn-oiled streets,
Only a kind of awe at his simple
Determination.
I can see him standing outside
A steaming Chinese diner, the leaves, wet
And sticking to his shoulders, his arms, his
Face, staring absently into the window
The way a man dreams
Someday he might live comfortably
Inside the mystery of his life. He watches
A man there chewing a leg of duck, the flesh falling
In easy slabs he swallows, wondering
If to live is to be trapped always
In the murderous loves of the body. But now
There is something that leads me out
Of the throbbing boulevards of memory
To cross the park, fog and moonlight
Dripping through the pines. In the distance
The sea breathing. And I feel the cold
Settle into my coat, the weathered husk I carry
Toward the lighted house.

# Everywhere the Light

I love the way in winter the light slips
      the slim bones of the trees
and sparks the lawn's thin filaments, how it
      pulls the mushrooms' heads, blind and fleshy,
from the fig's arthritic feet. Everywhere
      in January the light seems thin
and cold. Even the square of it the window's chopped
      and hung on the wall
trembles a little, the way the pale expanse
      of a woman's back

shudders to a lover's touch. Today I watch it draw my neighbor,
      at 80 slow and brittle
as dead leaves, out on her patio to sing lullabies
      to her cat who blinks casually
as if he preferred opera and in Italian.
      I have not forgotten how I
was entertained as a child by the old man
      dying next door.
He'd sit in his yard, in what was left
      of the body that rotted

around him like a piece of bad fruit. And while
      I watched he'd wink,
and stuff the butt of a Camel filter into a hole,
      no more the thickness
of a child's finger, slit by surgeons in his throat.
      Mostly I remember
how he closed his eyes when he did it.
      How it gave him
pleasure. Once, in a voice that sounded
      like kitchen matches scratched

On concrete, he said to me, Cancer isn't an evil thing,
      boy. It just is. It wants
to live like anything else. And he gestured
      toward his garden and the trees there
splintered by light. And so in my life I have looked

for the small pleasure:
trees, rain, the simplicity of light as it glances
off the face of a building,
whatever is offered as I too am pulled
toward what I cannot name.

# Three Times I Petition the Sky

Why did the good doctor go on with those cards, the useless questions?
I'd already told him they were nothing but inkblots. Or
the spot on my lungs. Moss on the white rock above
treeline. What I see when I close my eyes.
Where we are going.

At dawn the red tiles of the roofs steam among the shafts of light.
In the distance, a great range of clouds supported by pillars of rain.
I rub the new scar on my Adam's apple, polishing
my solitude like a new possession. In the quiet
I shuffle memories like photographs; held by one.
Did we really stand on that shore
with those birds whose small cries and broken tracks
the winds erased?

Venus is drowsing in a thicket of stars. Geese
stitch a dark line across the sky. Why
now, with this woman, in this place
do I take up my life, and walk?

# Hummingbird

After the sudden storm,
traffic hisses over sun-
flooded streets, leaves
pasted on the tires,
the gutters swirling.
I walk down the sidewalk,
my heart balanced
on the twin blades of
gratitude and fear.
The girl behind
the drugstore counter
calls me, Sir, the dead
shimmer of her
green contacts passing
through me to the
window and a sky, swirled
the color of grease
gone cold in a skillet.
She could be my sister,
at her age already
married to a man who
felt more keenly than
most the soft collapse
of our culture.
Reading murder in
the eyes of his neighbors,
he ran into the street,
one day, thrusting his
head through the windshield
of a passing Chevy. Now
when I see her, her eyes
seem somehow splintered.
Yesterday
I sat in the park
watching the willows
shiver, the wind
playing in them like
a hand sliding into

a silken dress, the flowers
exploding noiselessly
in a ring of fire, a
hummingbird there, darting
in and out of the flame, its
tiny, metallic body
tracing a brief
memory of light across
the lens of the eye.
I sat on my bench
as the shadowed
clock in its tower
groaned, the wheels
humming as it arced
its hands towards noon.
I knew then, that soon,
the woman I need
would come from
the office she hates. And
I would take into
my arms this life, moving
with its silent whir and
flooded heart, its needle
flashing.

# III

*For seven years I have known*
*this sickness, the winded birch*
*that flogs the window, the cruelty*
*of light. I dream on my feet, eyes*
*wreathed with the white flies of exhaustion.*

# Beauty

The sky, a thickening mirror I watch, groans
With the stubborn sounds of a chained stump
Ripped from soil. And I feel within me
The cyst of a prayer that has hardened for years
Pulse with blind insistence. Perhaps
Beauty is an image projected, the luminous clouds
I stared into as a boy, burning
My eyes.
       It was years ago
Under the vague, dirtied paint, curling
From the ceiling of a two-hundred-dollar apartment
That I grew quiet in the sudden
Absence of her dress, almost holy,
Watching what was left of the sunlight
Striping the mattress and the solemn
Curves of her shoulders. I traced
The long question that scarred her
Belly, swollen like a vessel of water
And placed her hand on my chest, pressing
Her finger, *There,* as if it could enter the blood
Streaking the walls of my heart.

       Somewhere in the distance
I heard a line of boxcars rush east
With the sureness of history, mindless
As the fear I carried for years. I imagined
The few men sitting crosslegged on top
Of that train, drowsy as buddhas, faces
Darkened with the muted
Ambitions of rust, riding that iron
Carcass, slippery with mud
And the rain's iridescence.
       I suppose later
They dropped from the cars, steaming
In the moonlit switchyards
Of a city in Kansas
Or Montana, the fading crunch
Of their boots on gravel, the sound

Of something like ice
Breaking apart.
                Once a boy
In a public urinal showed me, I guess
In what was the loneliness of adolescence, his
Penis. I was strung there
In the raw silence of the high windows,
A few flies buzzing lazily, feeling
Sickened, not by his
Presumption but by the emptiness
Of his offer. Something
In the ragged landscape of his face
Reminded me of the hunger my
Mother had once shown me
In the paintings of saints.
                That was
A long time ago.
I tell you there is a student now,
In one of my classes. When she laughs
The faces of young men grow still as
Pools of rain a cold wind has passed
Over. Yesterday I saw her
Dressed in the thin light of summer, coils of silver
Around one ankle. I try to touch her,
Late at night, with these fingers
Of type striking paper. Do you see?
I hate her. She is moving too quickly.
She wears red ribbons in her hair.

# Eyes of Winter

Lying here before sleep
I watch the shadows
Of branches bowing
Heavily to the winter wind,
And think of you again
In that empty barn
Hanging like wet laundry,
Your throat closed, your eyes
Inflated as if startled
At their first sight of oblivion.
I remember the owl
Perched in the rafters
Twisting its head, shifting
From one foot to the other,
Finally lifting through the holes
Shotgunned in the roof.
Now in your sons
Sleeps an unrootable
Question, curling them
Where they dream
Side by side, as if stirred
By the moon's blank face
Arcing across the window.

I was stunned by your widow
Poised in her sorrow and dark dress
Like one rose balanced in a vase,
Her lips, carefully etched, explaining
That she had to accept
And forget in order to live,
Mouthing the smooth language
Of therapy. Yet something in her was moving
Behind her eyes
Gathering toward its end,
Perhaps the shuddering morning
Stars slowing to a halt
With the steel sound of a train
But higher, the sound of grief,
A pitch too high and pure
For me to hear.

# Prayer for the Living

They are standing there, fleshed in the false light
Of the streetlamps, wrapped
In the fresh silence of morning, waiting
For a cab, I suppose, or bus, though none will come
At an hour like this. A boy
And his mother, too heavy for her knees
Or the frail splayed bones of her feet, so she leans
On an aluminum cane, the boy,
Shuffling and tense, young enough to be a little ashamed
Of his mother, but worried too, for her, one half
Of his face scrunched up as if it were sewn,
As if the threads of love pulled too tight
This time and hurt him and left his face
Looking like that, sort of curious but dumb.

Why don't they just phone someone?
Maybe another son, the older brother,
The one, perhaps, they've come to visit.
He could be middle aged and successful,
Sliding up in a warm El Dorado. Maybe
He's dead and *they've* come for *him.*
Maybe that's why they look so stunned.
Somebody's gone, swallowed up by something
As everyday and inexplicable as death, gone
Back into the shape air makes when
Nothing is there.

Christ, I'm tired of this: 2000 miles
Of mountains and ice, the cities
All boxed and the same, the days
That have fallen like leaves, me
Standing here now like
A mannequin in the window
Of an Easy 8 Motel.
I have my own to bury today.

The few cold stars have faded
And the sun's up. Jesus, that's good.

60

Somebody will come or the phone will ring
With a voice human and full, and
That's good. That's enough, when you're tired, burnt
Down to your center and clear
Tired of this waiting and missing somebody.

# On the Morning of Your New Life

Tear the pages from your journal,
The sudden blood that stains
Your bedsheets, tear memory
And sorrow as you would
Skin from the bone.

Let your eyes close and you will see
The little hole of fear
That opens like a dark flower
Back in the brain.
You must not listen too closely
To its awful singing.

You must gather the faces
Of those you love
And come slowly to the burning
Window, the ragged light
That makes it possible.

# The Wrecking Yard

Today I wander here
for a missing part
beneath a receding Sunday sun
that sparks at the edges of windows
and bristles from a thousand antenna
tips: a February sun, too distant now
to offer any warmth.
Here what's left of the rain is strung
in the long ruts of the roadway
as the day hurries toward dusk and the wind
bangs off the rotting fences.
Here, the giant metaled bodies,
collapse and decompose
like rows of beached whales:
Volkswagens, Plymouths, battered
Chevrolets, cock-eyed and strewn
like so many crumpled shoes. There's even
one elongated limo rutted in mud — with no
bride stepping out into sun, no groom, hungover,
tentative, almost happy.

Day laborers, black gloved and hooded,
grunt as they heave cracked batteries
leaking in the corner of the yard. On the far
side of the freeway children fling a lime green Frisbee
where the lush sourgrass has welcomed the rain.
They stop, and watch the clouds build
and dismantle their dark mosques.
Two women in yellow slickers, glimpse
under a crinkled hood, draw back as if bitten,
laugh and touch and turn away.
And I walk away
skirting the edge of the fences, tipped
with a gaunt scroll of razor wire.

A tin shed shucks the last light.
Wind buckles a tarp
strapped to the red husk of a Ford.

It is as if a great crowd converged here
once, abandoning their beloved automobiles
to walk out to meet some final wind, full
and blowing like Rapture, though I know nothing
is as simple as that. All I am sure of
is these few stars, like tiny flames
above saints in cathedrals, rising
up to the blackness that is theirs.

# The Fine Art Cinema

The projectionist's lamp stabs the screen
And the redhead who pirouettes
Once and steps out of her jeans, pooled
On the floor. Then the men in their sunken
Silence shift a little, eyes as wide
As those I have seen in church staring
At the grave images of saints, though these aisles
Smell of urine and rain. The falling column
Of light swirling with smoke seems to pulse
As she slides onto a sofa, the curve of her
Shoulders, the curve of her hips, the half-lidded
Eyes with tiny black centers tunneling
The vacancy of her body. In the empty
Hush I press my head back deeper
Into the seat watching the small, domed lights
Suspended overhead in the ceiling
Like dim stars, a few spiders dangling
Within their sticky constellations.

       It was in the new
Blush of a morning in 1973 when I moved
In the shallows of a young girl's hips. I recall
In her eyes something serious and dark
As the wet almonds I picked
One summer in a sunlit, windless field,
A trance-like sleep there, where the dreamers
Do not stop falling until they wake
Remembering the heat pressing the body, the gnats,
Another day persisting. There I woke to the sounds of her
Mother in the next room, drunk and struggling
To force a few mangled chords
From the keys of an organ, feeling
The intense concentration as she slowly
Counted time.

       That was the same year
One of my roommates who had been
Adopted as an infant told me *his* mother, thinned also

By years of gin would quiet
His outbursts by dialing the orphanage's
Telephone number. Once, when she found him slicing
The throats of frogs, she swore that his real mother
Had been a murderer. He said watching those tiny
Green bodies lurch and strangle in the grass
Had made something in him open and feel
Closer to nature.
           We were nineteen then
When his girl left him, shriveled by doubt and amphetamines; he
Drifted untethered, letting his hair grow, never
Washing, his face transformed into a kind
Of smudged erasure. Sitting here now, I don't know
What it is we require. Perhaps a pair of eyes looking back
When we look out. The redhead is standing
Up now, lifting a small, honey-colored boxer
To the camera, our vision narrowed toward the animal's
Dripping genitalia. We are left with this image frozen, scarcely
Blurred by the credits as we empty into the wind
Sweeping over the graveled parking lot, the bits of broken
Glass and chewing gum wrappers. And as I edge the car
Into these streets trafficking in lawn chairs and televisions,
Shotguns and liquor, I know only
That we have paid and will again,
If only to see.

# Near Treeline

This is the wind's
high winter encampment
where a black hawk maps
invisible thermals
above the snow
and the streambed's polished rock.
I crest a hill and come upon
a stand of naked trees, totems
carved by wind and fire. The sun
a red coal now, begins to sink
into its bed of ash. I don't
want to sleep in this place.
It reminds me too much
of the dream
that followed me here
last summer — a plunging
appaloosa dragged down
by the steaming mouths of wolves,
by morning the wings
of the shoulders, opened
and glowing
with a robe of ants. Still
I come here again and again,
even in winter,
drawn by the frail light
ground into the fields
of granite, by whatever
is in me that wants to know
more than it can. I remember
the journals of the obscure
Norwegian explorer
I read as a child, how once
he shot his horse, slit
it open and crawled in
to keep from freezing.
I used to imagine
the eyes of that horse swiveling
back, huge and curious

when it felt the barrel
of the revolver rest
against its temple.
Afterwards, he wrote,
the Inuit welcomed him —
*the man who dreams*
*of galloping*
*in his house of blood.*

# Jimmy Finds-A-Feather Speaks For Me

Half crazed with winter
and the promise of spring
the dogs set out, mapping
the zig-zag scent of rabbit
or squirrel, the dry grass,
a dead sea their heads
bob in. Jimmy and I skirt the edge
of Raymond's Quarry, carved
by dynamite and diamond wire,
following the dogs down
the rock terraces
cut into the hillside.
We can hear them below
us, their cries rising
out of the empty
throat of the mountain.
Jimmy's full-blooded Miwok
with long thin hair
he knots in a black rosette
at the base of his neck.
And he moves quickly,
so that we drop, panting,
near bones of a deer, clouds
of insects settling
on the strange daffodils
blooming from the jaws. We
watch dusk begin its purple
crumbling, black letters
of geese fanning overhead.
Jimmy says the wind is breathing.
It's not wise to linger here
in the scars of the earth.
He says he has seen the grief
in my face
since the child was taken,
and his voice has a fullness

beneath it that makes
what he says something
you listen to. Once, near here,
he crawled through
buck brush and manzanita
hunting grasshoppers for bait
and found a speckled fawn
shuddering with fear
in a basket of grass.
It blinked at him
with great dragonfly lashes
and made his heart
shrink. I was, he says,
at the very center of things.
And when it raised
its neck and turned
away from me
looking at what light
was left shining in the trees,
I looked with it
so that when I turned
back it was gone.
It was like that,
wasn't it? he says.
Yes, I say, like that.

# The Marrying Poem

I watch the autumn leaves
Wheel down like moths
Or the spotted hawks
I've seen in their hunger
Drop into the distance.
Now I know love can come
To live inside you
Long after you stopped
Wanting it. And it can
Press the sore places
There until water and
Salt come, unasked for,
To the center of your eyes,
The way it did the first
Time you brought down
A bird and opened it
And touched — the liver,
The slick intestines,
The gray muscled heart.

It is what kept me
Standing there in town,
In the mirror's three
Versions of myself,
Measured for the second
Suit I've owned, beautiful
enough to marry. Now
Shadows of clouds
Buckle over the grass.
They bring no rain
And still the ground
Lies cracked and open.
Birds pass their seeds
And the red clay
Takes them. A woodpecker
Knocks and a few squirrels
Quarrel in the dying
Oak. You could look back
And call it luck.

# One Day at a Time

There's a man I know smoking
in the dark across the street,
his hotbox pulsing in the 2 a.m. stillness.
He's drained another bottle of gin and is sinking
into the lowest layers of himself.
I used to sit like that
until the jars of wine were spent
and my thoughts slowed,
until the dark air grew warm on my face,
and the pupils of my eyes swelled.

        One morning I woke
with a bubble of blood in the corner
of my eye, the woman gone, the window
looming where a sparrow lay
with a broken neck. I took it as a sign.
And gave myself up. Now if you see me
groping my way through a sunlit avenue
in California, my mole eyes slitted shut, my coat
dragging its iron shadow, you'll see I'm walking,
almost upright, a clerk, into the new world.

# Blood Rings

Early in a blue dawn, great slabs of rain
Slid twisting over the eaves of the barn

Like schools of minnows catching the light. Now clouds
Shadow the grass, their ghostly footprints

Climbing the hillside, cooling
The backs of field-rock and cattle. And

I am grateful for what sun is left, dropping
Its soft ropes over me. Sometimes, afternoons like this

The wind will mutter in the low tones my father used. Strange
How his voice can still rise

Suddenly in my head like the smell of rain
Or wood. All his life he walked away from something

With the slow resolve of a fist
Closing. A silence sweating in a glass jar.

An ancient moss
Brocades these stones someone piled on the hilltop

Where a raven graphs his circle of hunger
Overhead. Once my father and I

Found a spider's nest
Beneath a heap of rocks like this. *Leave it,*

Was all he said. But that spring I overturned
The slate that roofed that widow's progeny

And struck a match and lowered it
Into those teeming bodies sucking inward,

Tiny white hands, curled and melting. I felt
A hair graze my hand, a needle's tearing

And two suns took my eyes
As what seemed a fistful of moths

Burst softly in my chest. I lived. Though
One hand still bears the mark, a tiny star

Whose orbit does not close. Some evenings
When the light drains and

Raven goes slowly home, my heart trots
A little more quickly within its ring of blood,

As the powdered dusk
Settles over me, silent as those wings.

*D. J. Smith was born in 1955 in Fresno, in the heart of California's great central valley, a brutal landscape which often informs his poems. He received his B. A. degree in Drama from California State University, Fresno, in 1979. He has worked as a clerk, truck loader, and stagehand, though primarily as a teacher. He returned to school, completing an M. A. degree in Counseling in 1989. Though sudden and complete, the lure of poetry came late; he was in his mid-thirties when he began to study with poets Peter Everwine, Corrinne Hales, Charles Hanzliceck, and Philip Levine, eventually taking an M. A. degree in Creative Writing at CSUF in 1994.* **Prayers for the Dead Ventriloquist** *( Ahsahta ) is his first collection, though individual poems have appeared in the U. S. and abroad. He is married and continues to work and write in Fresno.*

# Ahsahta Press

## MODERN & CONTEMPORARY POETRY
## OF THE AMERICAN WEST

Sandra Alcosser, *A Fish To Feed All Hunger*
David Axelrod, *Jerusalem of Grass*
*David Baker, *Laws of the Land*
Dick Barnes, *Few and Far Between*
*Conger Beasley, Jr., *Over DeSoto's Bones*
Linda Bierds, *Flights of the Harvest Mare*
Richard Blessing, *Winter Constellations*
*Peggy Pond Church, *New & Selected Poems*
Katharine Coles, *The One Right Touch*
Wyn Cooper, *The Country of Here Below*
*Judson Crews, *The Clock of Moss*
H. L. Davis, *Selected Poems*
*Susan Strayer Deal, *The Dark Is a Door*
　　　　　　　　　　*No Moving Parts*
*Gretel Ehrlich, *To Touch the Water*
Gary Esarey, *How Crows Talk and Willows Walk*
Julie Fay, *Portraits of Women*
*Thomas Hornsby Ferril, *Anvil of Roses*
　　　　　　　　　　*Westering*
*Hildegarde Flanner, *The Hearkening Eye*
Charley John Greasybear, *Songs*
Corrinne Hales, *Underground*
Hazel Hall, *Selected Poems*
Nan Hannon, *Sky River*
Gwendolen Haste, *Selected Poems*
Kevin Hearle, *Each Thing We Know Is Changed Because We Know It
　　　　　　　　　　And Other Poems*
Sonya Hess, *Kingdom of Lost Waters*
Cynthia Hogue, *The Woman in Red*
*Robert Krieger, *Headlands, Rising*
Elio Emiliano Ligi, *Disturbances*
Haniel Long, *My Seasons*
*Norman Macleod, *Selected Poems*
Ken McCullough, *Sycamore•Oriole*

Barbara Meyn, *The Abalone Heart*
Dixie Partridge, *Deer in the Haystacks*
Gerrye Payne, *The Year-God*
George Perreault, *Curved Like An Eye*
Howard W. Robertson, *to the fierce guard in the Assyrian Saloon*
*Leo Romero, *Agua Negra*
               *Going Home Away Indian*
Philip St. Clair, *At the Tent of Heaven*
               *Little-Dog-Of-Iron*
Donald Schenker, *Up Here*
Gary Short, *Theory of Twilight*
D.J. Smith, *Prayers for the Dead Ventriloquist*
*Richard Speakes, *Hannah's Travel*
Genevieve Taggard, *To the Natural World*
*Marnie Walsh, *A Taste of the Knife*
Bill Witherup, *Men at Work*
*Carolyne Wright, *Stealing the Children*

*Women Poets of the West: An Anthology, 1850-1950*

*Selections from these volumes, read by their authors, are available on *The Ahsahta Cassette Sampler.*